Surviving ObamaCare

*Money Saving Solutions
For Today's Health Care Crisis*

I0101785

MATTHEW IRONS

M.I. Publishing

ISBN-13: 978-0615798790
ISBN-10: 0615798799

CONTENTS

CHAPTER 1:
INTRODUCTION

Thank you so much for your interest in this book. It is a humbling experience to write a book on such a broad topic as health insurance and more specifically healthcare reform.

I want to say on the outset, I am swimming in the deep end of the pool. The healthcare reform law was a whopping 2700 page document which then has grown to 20,000 pages as of this writing. I also want to clarify that this book is not meant to be an exhaustive explanation on the fine details of the health reform law. Rather, this book will focus more on money saving solutions once everything gets underway beginning in 2014.

Why did I write this book? A lot of the books I have read did a great job of identifying and navigating through the confusing verbiage that is included in the health reform law, commonly known as ObamaCare.

Being a health insurance agent, my job has always been about helping my community find quality health insurance coverage at an affordable price. My main role is to provide solutions to problems. The motto of my office is H.O.P.E, which means Helping-Other-People-Everyday.

This book is an attempt to provide you with solutions on how to save the most money during the new age of health insurance called ObamaCare.

We need to begin our journey with a core foundation so we get a clear understanding of what health insurance is. That way we are on the same page as far as fundamental concepts and definitions. We will discuss the reasons why we need health insurance and why it is an important vehicle to secure our financial well-being.

As a health insurance agent the most common question I have is in regard to the specific terms and definitions used in the world of health insurance. I like to call it our own secret language. I say this because a lot of my customers are baffled as to what each of the terms mean and how it will impact them on a day to day basis. I will reveal and decode the secret language of health insurance so you will be equipped to make the best healthcare decisions for you and your family.

We will transition from fundamentals and examine the time-line of the health reform act and how it will impact American citizens for the good and the bad. I know this topic can get very heated and I will do my best to stay as bipartisan as possible. However, the facts are the facts; and we do need to take an honest look as to the financial impact we are all going to face. Things will not just go away if we ignore the issues. That would be a sure plan for financial ruin.

Once we identify the financial ramifications of the bill. We will examine the different healthcare options available once ObamaCare is in force.

Finally, we will identify money saving solutions to survive the new world of health reform. We will explore the mandated options and how we can best evaluate which plan will be a good fit for you or your family. What happens if the mandated plans are too expensive? Do we have anything else, or are we doomed to go uninsured risking our financial security in the event of a catastrophe? I will reveal unconventional plan options that will provide comprehensive coverage at a fraction of the cost.

What about business owners? Under the new health reform laws, business owners now have more responsibility than ever which will expand the cost of doing business at an almost crippling rate. I will show how business owners can be heroes in the eyes of their employees and provide solutions that will put money back into the business.

Business owners drive our economy and create jobs. By using these strategies, their success will be solidified and a win-win scenario between the employer and employee relationship will be created.

With that said, let's roll up our sleeves and get down to the business of entering the exciting world of health insurance.

CHAPTER 2:
BUILDING THE FOUNDATION

In this chapter, we are going to tackle the fundamentals of health insurance. I know what you are probably thinking, "BORING!" I understand your concern and I will work hard not to put you into a reading induced coma. I will try and keep my thoughts swift and to the point so we can get to the good stuff of how to save money.

Health insurance in itself is a very broad topic. It contains many subsections, rules and regulations that are outside of the scope of this book. The purpose of this chapter is to provide laser targeted information specifically on underage (under the age of 65) major medical insurance as it relates to the major tenets of ObamaCare. I will answer questions like, what is health insurance; and, why do we need health coverage?

As with any subject, we need to build upon a strong foundation which provides a solid basis regarding a particular subject. With a solid baseline, we can be on the same page when we develop more complex concepts. With this in mind, we need to answer the fundamental question, what is health insurance?

What Is Health Insurance?

The most basic definition of health insurance, or any insurance for that matter, is trading a small known risk (a premium or payment) and invest it to prepare for a possible larger unknown risk. In other words, you pay a small known monthly premium/payment (the small risk) to an insurance company to provide financial security for the possible unknown larger risk like a broken arm, or heart attack.

Health insurance can be reduced to two core principles; the first core principle is pre-paid medical services. This is, paying an affordable monthly payment that is used to provide security in the event of a medical emergency. The second core principle is being a part of a group or network to receive discounted rates for medical services. Typically, you are eligible for these types of savings if you are included in a major medical program called managed care plans. The most common forms of managed care plans are Preferred Provider Organizations, more commonly known as PPO plans and Health Maintenance Organizations also known as HMO plans.

What is Major Medical Insurance?

Major Medical insurance evolved from a type of health insurance plan called basic medical expense policies around the 1950's. Many of these basic expense policies did not provide enough protection for major or catastrophic medical expenses.

Originally, major medical insurance was created to provide protection for the larger medical bills while the client paid for the smaller or routine medical expenses out of their own pocket. Over time, major medical insurance would evolve again into comprehensive major medical insurance. This provides coverage for the smaller routine expenses as well, like doctor visits and prescription medication.

Major medical health insurance is broadly defined into two major categories, individual plans and employer group plans. In order to keep focus on ObamaCare, I want to paint in broad stokes because these two types of plan categories are going to be impacted the most by health care reform.

What Are Group Health Insurance Plans?

Group health insurance plans are provided by an association or employer. Most states constitute a group as at least two or more people who have a common association that is not formed for the sole purpose of obtaining health insurance. This definition can also include members of a union, professional association, and alumni associations.

Group health insurance plans exploded in popularity in the World War II era. At that time, the workforce demanded to be paid more. Unfortunately, because America was currently at war, paycheck increases were not able to be granted because of wartime wage and price controls.

In an effort to help the labor force without breaking the rules, Congress exempted employer health insurance plans from wage controls and taxation. This basically provided the opportunity for employees to get a raise in the form of non-taxed health insurance.

As a result, employers' experienced a generous tax advantage by providing health coverage on a "pre-tax" basis verses buying health insurance after taxes were deducted from a paycheck. This became a win-win scenario, employers received tax breaks while employees now had access to affordable medical insurance.

What Are Individual Health Insurance Plans?

If someone is not able to obtain health insurance from an employer or association then the individual can get health insurance directly from an insurance company. This provides a number of benefits. One major benefit is the individual does not have to worry about losing health insurance if he or she leaves a job. They can take the insurance where ever they go, it is portable. Also, in some cases an individual plan can be more affordable compared to a group plan if the group is small or if some members suffer from a pre-existing condition.

However, individual plans are underwritten. Meaning, insurance companies evaluate how healthy a person is when they apply for coverage. This can result in restricted coverage through what is called an exclusion rider. Also, a person can be declined altogether if they suffer from a major pre-existing condition. This is one of the major reasons why health reform is here today.

Why Do We Need Health Insurance?

I'm sure the answer to this question seems obvious, but it needs to be addressed. You know the old saying, "Whatever can go wrong probably will?" Well, that is why health insurance is so important. Everyone would like to think they are invincible and will never have any medical issues; however, we all do some time or another. Health insurance allows people to get the quality care they need when they need it most.

When you have a medical issue, your insurance pays for it, or at least a good percentage of it. All you have to do is pay your monthly premium, submit proof of the procedure, and pay your responsibility of the bill in the form of a deductible and/or copay.

Health insurance may not seem affordable, as the monthly premiums keep increasing year after year, but when there is a health emergency, you'll be happy you had coverage.

Many of my clients call me with their experiences. One of my clients cracked their head on a counter top and needed to go to the emergency room. With any head injury, the hospital will generally perform a CAT scan and other tests to be sure there is no internal brain damage. If my client did not have health insurance, the bill would have been over $2600 dollars! Thankfully my client had a great policy and they only paid approximately $500.

But why do 46 million Americans still have no health insurance? There are a variety of reasons, including affordability. However, the main reason is that they do not see the value of it or do not believe they will need it. No one is invincible. Anyone can get sick or have an accident resulting in an injury. This is why it is important to be prepared for any situation.

The truth is, we are just one claim away from filing bankruptcy. Do you know why most people file bankruptcy? We would assume it was due to credit card bills or defaults on loan payments. These are major contributors, but the major reason why people file bankruptcy is due to medical bills!

A study done in 2005 indicated that up to 1 million middle class families file bankruptcy each year due to medical bills. The sad part is, many of these families had some form of health insurance, but they were not properly or adequately insured. This is why we need a good understanding of the fundamentals so we do not fall into these financial pitfalls. A bankruptcy can devastate your financial standing for at least seven years preventing many families from buying their dream home or starting their own business[1].

So why are we discussing the importance of health insurance in a book about ObamaCare? Doesn't the bill say that we are all going to get coverage once everything is in place? On the surface yes, more Americans will have access to health insurance. However, as we dig deeper in understanding what our options are, we will discover that not all health insurance plans are created equal and can have a wide range of protection for the policy holder.

CHAPTER 3:
UNDERSTANDING
THE SECRET LANGUAGE OF
HEALTH INSURANCE

If you are confused about health insurance terms and scratch your head when you are evaluating policies or quotes, then this chapter is for you. I will admit health insurance is not easy. Have you ever felt like your insurance agent is speaking another language?

I have heard a number of times that people are more confused after a meeting with their health agent than before. To better understand what your choices are, you need to know key terms and definitions in order to choose the right health insurance plan for your family.

For the purposes of this book, the terms below will allow us to be on the same page of understanding as we unpack more information about health insurance before and after ObamaCare.

⅄ **Premium:** Your monthly, quarterly, or annual payment for insurance coverage.

⅄ **Deductible:** The pre-set amount of money that needs to be paid before a medical bill will be paid by the insurance company. Deductible amounts vary and are outlined in your policy.

⅄ **Coinsurance:** Generally, in any insurance claim after you pay your deductible, the insurance company pays a percentage of the bill. Usually the insurance company pays 80% and you pay the remaining 20%. You would see this in your policy as an 80/20 coinsurance.

⅄ **Maximum Out-of-Pocket:** The maximum out of pocket cost that you would pay after your deductible and coinsurance. The maximum out of pocket cost vary from each insurance company.

⅄ **Co-payment:** A small payment to see your family doctor or emergency room visit.

⅄ **Covered Expenses:** The items or services that the insurance company would pay for in the event of an occurrence. Most insurance companies do have limitations on what their policy will cover. Be sure to review your outline of benefits to see what is included in your plan.

⅄ **Exclusions:** Specific items that are not covered in your insurance policy.

⅄ **Pre-existing Condition:** A health problem that occurred before you had insurance coverage.

⅄ **Waiting Period:** The set amount of time before a preexisting condition will be covered by your insurance company. The waiting periods vary between insurance companies.

⅄ **Claim:** This is the medical bill for services rendered at a doctor's office or hospital.

⅄ **Provider:** A doctor, hospital or any other medical professional

⅄ **Network:** A group of doctors and hospitals that have a contract with an insurance company.

⅄ **Out-of-Network:** Any doctor or hospital that is not contracted with the insurance company. Usually, if you see a doctor or go to a hospital that is not within your network, the insurance company will pay a different amount. Generally, your deductible is increased and the coinsurance may change from 80/20 to 60/40 or even 50/50.

CHAPTER 4:
WHAT ARE THE CHANGES?

With anything new there can be a lot of anxiety. I can remember when I first got married how terrified I was. Questions raced through my mind... Was I going to be a good husband? How will I provide for my family? What investments do I need to have in place to secure my future?

Then, we had children! Again, this shot fear through my bones and propelled more questions. At any rate, once the initial fear subsided and the chaotic fog faded away, I started to learn the rules of the game. I will admit I am still learning, however, everything starts with a single step.

The same is true as it relates to ObamaCare. The issues with health care reform have caused a lot of anxiety, fear, and questions most of which include:

- Will we still have access to top notch health care?
- How much will it cost and can we afford the new coverage?
- Will we continue to have control? Or will it be tied up in bureaucratic red tape?

Whether we like it or not, ObamaCare is here to stay. The next few chapters will attempt to answer the questions relating to ObamaCare and how we can save the most money. For now, let's uncover some of the areas that ObamaCare will change.

1. Individual mandate of coverage: This is one of the most controversial areas of the new law. The law states that everyone will be required to have "qualified" health insurance or be subject to a tax.

2. Dependent children are able to stay on their parents' plan until the age of 26.

3. Health insurance companies can no longer cancel policies if anyone gets sick or severely injured. The only exception to this is in the event of fraud.

4. Health insurance plans can no longer have lifetime maximums.

5. Health insurance plans can no longer have annual maximums.

6. Health insurance plans must provide 100% coverage for preventative care and wellness procedures

7. People with pre-existing conditions will no longer be denied coverage due to their medical history.

8. People with pre-existing conditions will pay the same rate as healthy policy owners.

9. States are encouraged to expand Medicaid

10. New mandated essential health benefits are required on "qualified" health insurance plans

11. Opening of a new health insurance exchange

12. New tax credits to subsidize premiums for low income earners.

What is the time-line for ObamaCare?

At the time of this writing, we are just approaching the precipice of the new health care law. However, we have experienced some changes already! Let's take a look and review what has already happened and examine what is to come:

- March 2010 President Obama signed the Patient Protection and Affordable Care Act.
- July of 2010 we experience the first wave of 18 new taxes and tax increases.

- September 2010 begins the first roll-out of mandates:
  - Major medical insurance companies are now required to pay 100% of preventative care.
  - Removal of annual and lifetime maximums to major medical policies.
  - Child dependents can stay on parents' plan until age 26
  - All emergency care must be considered "in network"
  - Major medical insurance cannot deny or exclude benefits for children ages 19 and under because of pre-existing conditions.

- January 2011 marks the beginning of closing the "donut hole" in Medicare part D.

- January 2011 institutes more penalties and taxes:
  - HSA plans have elevated consequences for disbursements.
  - Medical device companies are assessed a tax
  - Pharmaceutical companies incur new fees.

- June of 2012 the US Supreme Court ruled the individual mandate as constitutional.

- January 2013 more taxes begin to roll-out:
  - A new 3.8% Tax on unearned income. This new tax targets capital gains in investment income.
  - New payroll tax increase for Medicare Part A

- Beginning January 2014 the next wave of mandates continue:
  - All Americans are required to have "qualified" health plans or receive a penalty
  - Employers with 50 or more employees are required to offer health insurance or receive a penalty
  - Insurance Companies cannot deny or exclude benefits for adults because of pre-existing conditions
  - Health Benefit Exchanges are open to the public.

- January 2018 and beyond:
  - New "Cadillac Tax" on benefit rich health plans
  - The Independent Payment Advisory Board (IPAB) begins to implement cuts in Medicare.

CHAPTER 5:
WHAT IS THE HEALTH
BENEFIT EXCHANGE?

A major facet of the health reform law is the implementation of a Health Benefit Exchange. In essence, the "Exchange" is a virtual shopping mall to buy health insurance. It allows consumers the ability to connect with health insurance companies and shop for coverage online, by phone, or in some cases retail establishments. Unless you are on Medicare, Medicaid, or eligible for an employer group plan, then you can shop at the Exchange.

What is the purpose of the exchange?

The purpose of the Exchange is two-fold: First, it monitors and controls the purchase of "qualified" health insurance plans. Second, it sets up the foundation for "SHOP", which stands for the Small-business Health Options Program.

The Exchange is also the vehicle in which people can receive a tax credit paid to the insurance company to help reduce the monthly premium. This tax credit is based on a sliding scale of your annual income up to 400% of the federal poverty line. Any consumer that exceeds the designated income level will not receive a subsidy at all and will be required to pay 100% of the premium themselves.

What plans will be available on the Exchange?

The Health Benefit Exchange will provide "qualified" health insurance plans that require a certain level of "essential benefits". Consumers will have a variety of insurance companies to choose from, but the coverage will be virtually the same. Health insurance plans will be designated in the following levels:

- **Bronze:** The Bronze plan will include mandatory essential benefits and pay an actuarial value of about 60 percent.

- **Silver:** The Silver plan will also include the mandated "essential benefits" and pay a value of about 70 percent.

- **Gold:** Just like the previous two plans, the Gold plan will include "essential benefits" and pay a coverage value of 80 percent.

- **Platinum:** The Platinum plan will pay a value of about 90 percent and will include the mandatory "essential benefits" as well.

The Health Benefit Exchange is not free from controversy. Many states have refused to set up their own exchanges. In these cases, the federal government will step in and create an exchange themselves. This may or may not be a good thing. If history serves as a good teacher, usually anything the government has control over usually ends up being cluttered with confusion and riddled with red tape.

In fact, as it stands right now the government's draft application is 15 pages long for a family of three. Plus, in addition to the IRS there will be three major federal agencies evaluating the submission of that application to validate your income, identity, and citizenship. This is only the beginning of the process. The first stage is to evaluate if you are eligible for tax credit assistance. The next stage is in selecting a plan. Huffington Post writes, "Applying for benefits under President Barack Obama's health care overhaul could be as daunting as doing your taxes"[2].

CHAPTER 6:
WHAT IS THE ESSENTIAL HEALTH BENEFITS PACKAGE?

In the previous chapter, we discussed the Health Insurance Exchange. One of the reasons why the exchange was created was to monitor and control the sale of "qualified" health insurance plans.

In this chapter, we will identify what constitutes a "qualified" plan. The Department of Health and Human Services, otherwise known as "HHS" stipulates that health insurance companies must provide a level of benefits that meet a specific "benchmark".

These benefit "benchmarks" cannot be changed or customized. To date, these "benchmarks" or levels of benefits still have not been determined. Currently, all we know is that health insurance plans must provide comprehensive coverage that includes 10 categories of coverage outlined in section 1301 and 1302 of the Affordable Care Act.

The Essential benefit categories are:

1. Emergency services

2. Ambulatory care

3. Hospitalization

4. Maternity coverage and newborn care

5. Mental health and substance abuse services

6. Coverage for prescription drugs

7. Rehabilitative devises and services

8. Lab work services

9. Wellness, preventative, and chronic disease management

10. Pediatric care, including dental and vision services

CHAPTER 7:
THE GOOD NEWS
AND THE BAD NEWS

To say the least the topic of ObamaCare can set people on edge. I think most Americans can agree that some form of health care reform was necessary. I'm not sure the new system is the best fit for our future; never the less, we need to understand its good points and its bad points.

Have you ever been in a situation where someone asks you, "Do you want the good news or the bad news first"? Well, whenever anyone asks me that question, I usually ask for the good news first. I guess it helps soften the blow of the bad news. Anyway, in this chapter I am going to begin with the "good news".

What is the Good news?

As I said earlier, I think Americans can agree that some level of healthcare reform was necessary. One of the major problems with the "old model" of health insurance is that it limited coverage or declined coverage for people with pre-existing conditions. This will no longer be an issue with the new changes implemented by ObamaCare.

People suffering with pre-existing conditions will enjoy the same benefits and pricing as a person with a healthy medical history. Additionally, insurance companies can no longer cancel policies if you get seriously injured or are chronically ill, except for circumstances of fraud.

As a health insurance agent, I am always asked to help people find affordable health insurance coverage. I love it when I am able to help people find a quality plan at a price that they can afford. However, sometimes families find great coverage, but the rate is just out of reach of their budget.

These families are struggling to get by, but make too much money to qualify for Medicaid. Unfortunately, in this scenario, they fall in between the gap of Medicaid and private insurance. With the expansion of Medicaid, this will be good news for these families as it will be a burden lifted off their shoulders allowing them to get some form of health insurance coverage.

And now... the bad news...

With the advent of ObamaCare, the "bad news" outweighs the "good news". One of the more controversial items within the law is section 1182 which in recent debates has shed light on the issue of what has been nicknamed, "death panels".

A sub-paragraph of 1182 authorizes the use of cost benefit analysis to calculate age, disability, and terminal illness. This law allows a medically untrained politician the power to limit the medical care your doctor may feel is necessary for your recovery. In other words, if you are too old and too sick, the government may restrict your medical care and leave you languishing for help.

Understanding the Consequences of Medicaid:

One of the largest tenants of the health reform law is the expansion of Medicaid. This is the major vehicle that will provide coverage for the uninsured in America. This expansion is a catch 22. As stated earlier, this is a good thing for people who fall between the cracks of Medicaid and private insurance. However, the consequences of this decision has wide spread ramifications.

The original purpose of Medicaid was not to be a permanent solution, but a temporary bridge to help individuals and families during hard economic times. With the new changes in ObamaCare, this is no longer true. Now if you earn up to 133% of the Federal

Poverty Line, you will be on Medicaid. Actuaries with the Centers for Medicare and Medicaid cautions that low income individuals and families who now have private insurance may lose it and be sent to Medicaid.

This is bad news for these individuals and families because more and more doctors are refusing to accept Medicaid patients. Studies have shown this will cause a massive rationing of care at local doctors' offices and hospitals, thus impacting the quality of healthcare these patients will receive[3]. Not only that, but historically research has proven Medicaid patients receive worse care even before the proposed expansion[3]. So now people with good coverage with a private insurance company may now be subject to sub-quality care because they are now forced to be on Medicaid.

In addition to the consequences created by the expansion of Medicaid, America will experience a much higher price tag for our medical care. We will receive new taxes, budget cuts for Medicare, increased rates, and penalties for individuals and small business owners.

CHAPTER 8:
HOW MUCH WILL IT COST?

As stated in the previous chapter, one of the biggest problems we are going to face with ObamaCare is the increased price tag. In this chapter, we are going to dig a little deeper and examine how much ObamaCare is going to cost.

Let's begin by going over the new taxes we will experience. Even though some of these taxes, tax increases, and limitations may not affect all of us directly, everyone at some point will indirectly feel the sting in our wallets. Think of it as a financial domino effect, starting from the top down.

New Taxes, Tax Increases, and Limitations[5]

⅄ 2.3% tax on medical device manufacturers

⅄ 10% tax on indoor tanning services

⅄ Blue Cross/Blue Shield tax hike

⅄ Excise tax on charitable hospitals which fail to comply with the requirements of ObamaCare

⅄ Tax on brand name drugs

⅄ Tax on health insurers

⅄ $500,000 annual executive compensation limit for health insurance rxecutives

⅄ Elimination of tax deduction for employer-provided retirement Rx drug coverage in coordination with Medicare Part D

⅄ Medicare tax on investment income 3.8% over $200k/$250k

⅄ Medicare Part A Tax increase of .9% over for anyone earning $200k/$250k

⅄ 40% Tax on "Cadillac" health insurance plans starting in 2018

⅄ An annual $63 fee levied by ObamaCare on all plans to help pay for insurance companies covering the costs of high-risk pools.

⅄ Over the counter limitations: Over the counter medicines no longer qualify as medical expenses for flexible spending accounts (FSAs), health reimbursement arrangements (HRAs), and health savings accounts (HSAs).

⅄ Additional tax on HSA/MSA distributions: Health savings account or an Archer medical savings account, penalties for spending money on non-qualified medical expenses. 10% to 20% in the case of a HSA and from 15% to 20% in the case of a MSA.

⅄ Flexible spending account cap 2013: Contributions to FSAs are reduced to $2,500 from $5,000.

⅄ Medical deduction threshold tax increase 2013: Threshold to deduct medical expenses as an itemized deduction increases to 10% from 7.5%.

⅄ Individual mandate (the tax for not purchasing insurance if you can afford it) 2014: Starting in 2014, anyone not buying "qualifying" health insurance must pay a surtax at a rate of 1% or $95 in 2014 to 2.5% in 2016 on income above the tax threshold. The total penalty amount cannot exceed the national average of the annual premiums of a "bronze level" health insurance plan on ObamaCare exchanges.

How will ObamaCare impact individuals?

    With the increase of additional taxes, more required benefits included in "qualified" health plans, limiting the rate for older policy owners, and including people with pre-existing conditions, insurance premiums have nowhere to go but up.

    Sources say that "Insurance premiums are set to explode. Already health insurers, citing the increased cost of various ObamaCare provisions, are seeking and winning double-digit premium hikes. For example, California health insurers are proposing increases for some customers of 20 percent or more: 26 percent by Blue Cross, 22 percent by Aetna, and 20 percent by Blue Shield"[6].

    Younger adults are facing the biggest increase of all with increases estimated at an average of 169%. In another study, the American Academy of Actuaries' magazine found that young adults that earn too much to receive subsidies will see an average rate increase of around 42%.

    Currently, the Congressional Budget Office estimates individuals will be paying approximately $5800 a year and a family of four will be paying around $15,200 a year by 2016[7]. With those calculations, individuals will be paying around $483 a month and $1266 a month for a family of four. Keep in mind, some individuals and families will receive subsidies to help with premium costs. However, that extra help from the government may not amount to much. The IRS has estimated premiums for a family of five to be around $20,000 dollars. Also, the IRS ruled that you are not eligible for subsidies if your employer offers you coverage with a group health insurance plan[6]. To get a clear picture of what you or your family may pay per month for health insurance you can visit:

http://healthreform.kff.org/subsidycalculator.aspx.

Needless to say, the word "affordable" in the Affordable Care And Protection Act may need to be revised by evidence of the devastating financial increases our country will face.

How will ObamaCare impact business owners?

Unfortunately, business owners will pay a heavy price for the new changes in our health care system. One of the new rules is that business owners with 50 or more employees are required to provide health insurance. If the business owner does not provide coverage, they will receive a penalty of $2000 per employee or $3000 per employee that receives tax subsidies from an exchange plan. Also, if the employee only portion of premium exceeds 9.5% of their pay the difference of that amount is passed back to the employer.

How will ObamaCare impact seniors?

More than half the costs of ObamaCare will be paid from reduced spending on seniors and people with disabilities who are on Medicare. According to Medicare's chief actuary, those that are covered by a Medicare Advantage plan will lose approximately $1267 in Medicare benefits in 2014 resulting in minimized coverage and increased monthly premiums. The actuary also states that one in every two Medicare Advantage members will lose their plan entirely.

Other Consequences?

In addition to the direct costs that seniors, individuals, and business owners will pay due to ObamaCare there are also other reactionary costs. Reactionary costs are indirect consequences made by the new increases.

It is estimated by actuaries that 14 million employees will lose their employer health insurance plan. The reason for this loss is due to the fact that the "tax" is about 1/7 of the cost of the estimated premiums that a business owner would be required to pay by the law. According to the National Center of Policy Analysis within 3 years of the new law, more than 100 million people will be forced into a health plan that will be more expensive and more regulated than the policy they currently have.

Currently, we are already seeing the impact of these changes. Employers are reducing wages, benefits and hours in order to afford the required health insurance coverage. Because of the extra burdens tethered to the backs of business owners, it could result in approximately 700 thousand lost jobs by 2019[8].

As stated in the previous chapter, there are devastating effects caused by the expansion of Medicaid. Because doctors and hospitals are getting paid less by Medicaid recipients, these providers are passing their losses on to private insurance companies resulting in increased premiums.

A study performed by Milliman & Roberson shows that private insurance premiums increased by $1500 a year as a direct result in the increases of Medicaid recipients. Keep in mind this study was performed before the changes outlined in ObamaCare. We can logically come to the conclusion that as a result of this expansion, insurance rates will skyrocket[9].

CHAPTER 9:
MONEY SAVING SOLUTIONS FOR INDIVIDUALS AND FAMILIES

Now that we have covered the general concepts of health insurance, outlined the major points of ObamaCare, and revealed the consequences we face by the impending law; we are now able to discuss the topic of how to save money. In this chapter, I am going to show you tips on how to save money on taxes, provide insight on how to save money on "qualified" plans, and offer suggestions of alternative coverage options if the "qualified" plans are too expensive or if you want better care than what Medicaid plans provide.

How to save money on taxes*:

As we discussed earlier in this book, ObamaCare has implemented a tax of 3.8% on unearned income.

---

* Seek advise from a qualified financial planner or attorney to determine your best options.

Examples of unearned income are: Dividends, capital gains, rental income, royalties, and proceeds from a sale of a home if it exceeds $250,000 for individuals and $500,000 for married couples. People impacted by this new tax are individuals earning more than $200,000 and people filing jointly earning $250,000 a year. In addition, trusts and estates that earn more than $12,000 will be impacted as well. If you fall into any one of these categories, below are some ideas on how to save money on this new tax.

1. Convert your traditional IRA into a Roth IRA. Roth IRA's are a "pay as you go" type of taxation model as opposed to traditional IRA's where you are taxed at the point of withdraw during retirement. By doing this conversion you will reduce your future taxable income.

2. Move assets into municipal bonds. Currently municipal bonds provide income that is exempt from federal taxes.

3. Invest in tax-favored vehicles like fixed indexed annuities. Money invested in annuities experience deferred taxation. This means, you will only pay taxes on your investment at the time of withdrawal. At the time of retirement, income should be below the surtax threshold.

4. Invest more into your SIMPLE IRA, SEP IRA, 401(k), or 403(b). By investing in these vehicles it will lower your earned income and withdraws will not be subject to the surtax because the IRS does not consider these returns as investment income.

5. If it is too late to convert your traditional IRA you can save money on the surtax by allocating your distributions to fund a life insurance policy.

6. Because the surtax will impact estates and trusts that earn $12,000 or more, speak with a skilled attorney. They will provide proper insight on how to manage your funds within these entities.

How to save money on health insurance:

In this new era of health insurance, "saving money" is going to take on a variety of forms which will depend on the individual. In my opinion, health insurance is not a "one size fits all" type of concept. Everyone experiences life differently and their situations are widely contrasted. Whenever anyone calls my office, I warmly thank them for the call and ask, "Tell me a little bit about your situation, how can I help you"?

The first step in finding the right plan is taking stock in your current situation and lifestyle. First off, if you earn below 133% of the poverty line, you won't get health insurance, you'll get Medicaid. You could be a young adult only needing coverage for the large catastrophic type of claim. You could be a family that needs full comprehensive coverage that includes doctor visits, lab work, and prescription medication. Or you could be a person suffering from a pre-existing condition and coverage in the past has either been non-existent or very expensive if you paid for coverage on your own. Like I said, everyone is different and each person needs coverage that fits best for their situation and lifestyle.

Another aspect in finding the right plan is to evaluate your medical history. How have you used your health insurance in the past? If you had a plan that included doctor visit co-pays, how many visits did you use last year? What was your annual deductible and did you satisfy it? These variables impacted the premiums of health insurance as it was before ObamaCare.

Even though, the options for coverage have been minimized, we can still use the same principles when selecting the "qualified" plans. For example, if you wanted more affordable premiums and are willing to give up some coverage, you could select the "bronze" plan in the exchange. Depending on your income level, you may qualify for a tax credit subsidy to help aid in the cost of premiums. Or, if you prefer more coverage and you are willing to pay more expensive premiums, then you could choose a more comprehensive plan like the "Platinum" option. Again, evaluate how you have used your health insurance in the past. This will help you determine what the best plan will be for you in the future.

To be fair, the best thing that has emerged from ObamaCare is the fact that people suffering with pre-existing conditions can now have affordable coverage. As an agent, this has always been the worst part of my job. I hated calling my clients and telling them that they were declined. You can imagine their fear and confusion as I broke the bad news.

Unfortunately, there were not many options to help. There was the "HIPPA plan", but the costs of those premiums were through the roof. Even though, ObamaCare does increase the rates for healthy people significantly, it does provide an affordable solution for people with pre-existing conditions when compared to "HIPPA plan" premium costs.

What if "qualified" plans are too expensive?

As we discussed in prior chapters, health insurance rates are set to skyrocket due to required increased "essential" benefits, expansion of Medicaid, and the inclusion of people with pre-existing conditions without underwriting. Because rates are going to be out of reach for many individuals and families, what are our options?

I guess the first "knee jerk" option is to go uninsured and wait until you need it. Some might feel this is the way to go, but I think this choice is very irresponsible and contributes to the increase of health care costs overall. Plus, what will you do when you wait to get coverage and then something happens? You are fully responsible for that claim and will pay everything out of your own pocket or file bankruptcy. Not only that, but you will be faced with the tax penalty and have nothing to show for it.

Off-Exchange Plan Options*

Thankfully there are other affordable options to meet your health care needs. "off-exchange" health insurance plans are not subject to the health reform mandates. These plans are underwritten to keep rates lower and do not cover unnecessary benefits as required in a "qualified" plan. These plan options are also a great affordable alternative for people that are subjected to the sub-standard care of Medicaid. Most of these plans use popular PPO networks allowing you to have access to doctors that may have refused to treat Medicaid recipients. With these plans you have freedom of choice!

Below are a couple examples of off-exchange plan types:

1. Fixed Benefit Indemnity Plans. These types of plans are very affordable and provide a fixed benefit amount for specific claims. For example, accidents, doctor visits, lab work, prescriptions, hospitalization among other benefits. There are a variety of plan types that range in benefit levels. Most of these plans are guaranteed renewable, meaning as long as you continue to pay your monthly premiums you will not lose coverage.

2. Sickness plans, accident plans, and first dollar wellness plans. Each of these types of plans are filed as separate policies; but when put together, they

---

* Check your state's regulations to review plan availability. Also speak with a licensed agent for a full evaluation of your needs.

provide coverage similar to a major medical plan, let's take a closer look at how this works (*see image #1*). When comparing these types of plans you can see the separate plans, when put together, provide similar coverage as a major medical plan. Each plan provides coverage for sicknesses, accidents, and wellness. Plus, both plan types share similar structure in that they have deductibles and coinsurance.

[*Image #1**]

Major Medical Insurance   Health Plan Not Subject To ObamaCare

Sickness Accident   Sickness   Accident

Wellness   Wellness

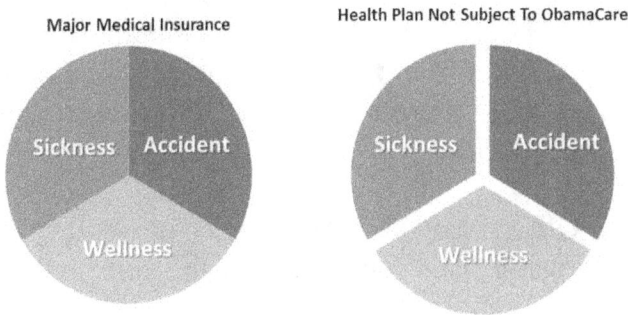

What about the penalty?

Because these plans fall outside the mandates of ObamaCare, you will be subject to the surtax for mandated coverage. This might seem hard to swallow; but, in reality the premiums of these plans are a fraction of the cost of "qualified" plans through the exchange. When factoring in the surtax and the savings in premiums, these health plans prove to be a more affordable option for your health care needs.

---

*   Example of a plan offered exclusively by USHealth Advisors

Also, most of these plans experience some form of rate guarantee which will lock in your premium for a least a year or more.

Are These Plans Legal?

Absolutely! Insurance is one of the most regulated industries in the United States. Every plan that is available to consumers must be evaluated and pass state regulations. Rest assured, if you select any plan that is "off-exchange", you will not be breaking any laws. Be sure when you are shopping for coverage, you select a plan from a company with a solid rating and long history within the health insurance marketplace.

"Off-Exchange" plans will prove to be more affordable than "qualified" plans from the exchange. Plus, the ability to obtain coverage will be a lot easier as well. As stated earlier in chapter 5, "in addition to the IRS there will be three major federal agencies evaluating the submission of the health insurance application to validate your income, identity, and citizenship. This is only the beginning of the process. The first stage is to evaluate if you are eligible for tax credit assistance. The next stage is in selecting a plan. Huffington Post writes, 'Applying for benefits under President Barack Obama's health care overhaul could be as daunting as doing your taxes[2]."

CHAPTER 10:
MONEY SAVING SOLUTIONS FOR THE
BUSINESS OWNER

The road for business owners will be a rocky one as
ObamaCare begins to unfold. Unfortunately, we will
be seeing more and more reductions in wages, hours,
and benefits, so owners will be able to afford the new
regulations of ObamaCare. Because of the new
increased healthcare costs, profits will erode and
impact the bottom line slowing company growth and
job creation. In this chapter, I will reveal ways
business owners can put money back into the business
to stimulate profits. This will allow the business the
ability to expand and provide more jobs.

Quick Review

Let's do a quick review of what business owners are
required to provide in ObamaCare. The law stipulates
in section 1513 that business owners with 50 or more
full time employees are required to offer health

insurance or receive a penalty of $2000 per employee or $3000 if the employee receives a tax credit through the exchange. In a group plan the owner is required by law to pay at least 50% of the "employee only" portion of the premium (business owners are not responsible for dependent premiums). If the employee's contribution of the "employee only" portion of the premium exceeds 9.5% then the business owner picks up the tab for the difference as well (dependent premium amounts are not calculated in this equation).

If a business owner has less than 50 full time employees then the owner is encouraged to provide group coverage through the SHOP program and receive tax credit subsidies to help compensate for the monthly premiums. This might sound like a good idea on the surface; but after careful evaluation, this could be very expensive for a business owner. Group health insurance premiums are estimated to be approximately $12,200 per employee[10]. Even with a tax credit, this is an overwhelming expense for the business owner.

So what are the options?

Option 1: Provide health insurance. I guess this could be the easy road out; but as we discussed, this choice is very expensive. The Congressional Budget Office estimates that employee health insurance premiums will be approximately $12,200.

Option 2: Stop offering group health insurance plans and have employees get coverage on their own. This is a somewhat better option for the business owner as they will not have the expensive price tag associated with the health insurance premiums. However, business owners with 50 or more employees will still be obligated to pay the reform mandated penalty of $2000 per employee or $3000 if the employee receives a tax credit through the exchange. Plus, the employer doesn't really get any benefit from paying this expense (tax). Normally, employers provide health insurance as a recruitment or retention tool to help compensate or reward employees. If the employer discontinues coverage, this may create tension within the workplace and possible employee fallout.

Option 3: Business owners can replace full-time employees with part-time employees. On the surface this option seems to solve the cost and mandate issues for the owner, but leaves the employees at a disadvantage. Employees would be forced to manage multiple part-time jobs in order to make financial ends meet. Also, because of this decision employees could be subject to Medicaid. Not only does this create more strain on the health care system in general, but will create poor moral within the workplace and harvest a lack of motivation from the employees. As a result it may diminish quality of service which could negatively impact profits for the business owner. Not only that, it may increase the employee turn-over rate which will cost the business owner thousands of dollars to recruit, hire, then train new employees.

At the risk of sounding like a late night infomercial, *"there's gotta be better way"!* The truth is, **THERE IS A BETTER WAY!**

Option 4: Whether you are a business owner with more than 50 employees or you are a small business with only 2 employees, this method will work for you! The best part is, your employees will think you are a hero! So what is this miracle solution? Option four is very similar to option 2 in that the employer will stop offering group health insurance coverage. However, there is a twist. What's this "twist" you may ask? I will spell it out for you in three letters, H-R-A.

Before we get into the details of an HRA, let me explain the advantages of this solution. If a business owner provides group health insurance, they are required by law to pay 50% of the "employee only" portion of the premium. As pointed out earlier, the Congressional Budget Office estimates the average employee premium to be $12,200. Because the employer ceases to provide group coverage this is will save the owner thousands of dollars a year.

The second advantage is for the benefit of the employee. The IRS just ruled that business owners are not responsible for covering the cost of dependents. Even though the "employee only" portion cannot exceed 9.5% of their income, the dependents' premium could be outrageous. If the business owner provides group health insurance, the dependents are not eligible to receive subsidies through the exchange forcing the cost of insurance to be unattainable. By having the business owner drop the group health insurance plan and have the employees find individual coverage, employees and their families may be eligible for tax credit subsidies through the exchange.

In the past, this was not always the best solution as group health insurance plans were "guarantee issue". This means that health insurance was guaranteed even if you had a pre-existing condition. If a business owner dropped the group coverage, employees with health problems would not be eligible for an underwritten individual plan leaving them uninsured and at risk. However, now with the new mandates of ObamaCare, people with pre-existing conditions can now get health insurance coverage the same as anyone who has a healthy medical history.

So what about the penalty?

If the business owner has less than 50 full-time employees, they will not be assessed the tax penalty. On the other hand, if the business owner has 50 full-time employees or more, then that business owner will have the penalty mandated by ObamaCare. However, we have a secret weapon to help with this penalty and provide assistance to your employees creating a win-win scenario. Its call an HRA!

CHAPTER 11:
THE BUSINESS OWNER'S SECRET WEAPON

What is an HRA?

An HRA stands for Health Reimbursement Arrangement. An HRA is an IRS program that is funded and managed by the business owner to help reimburse employees' medical expenses. What's great about this program is that 100% of these funds are tax deductible for the business owner and tax-free for the employee. Business owners have complete control over how this program is structured. There are no minimums or maximums in regard to how much money the business owner can allocate to their employees.

How Does The HRA Fit With Our ObamaCare Solution?

As we discussed in the previous chapter, it may be in the best interest for the business owner and the employee to drop the group health insurance plan. By dropping coverage, the business owner saves money on the expensive premiums every month and the employee benefits by having access to an individual plan through the exchange. Depending on the employee's income level, they could be eligible for a subsidy to help with the premium costs. The major area of concern is in regard to the penalty the employer would face if they have over 50 full-time employees. An HRA will help solve this problem.

One of the eligible medical expenses a business owner can reimburse for is health insurance premiums. For example, let's say the business owner provides every full-time employee $200 a month to help pay for individual health insurance either on or off the exchange. The employee receives $200 every month TAX-FREE and the employer gets a $200 a month tax deduction.

Also, a business owner can provide different benefit amounts to different classes of employee. For instance, a single employee can receive $200 a month while an employee plus dependents could receive $300 a month to help aid in the cost of individual health insurance.

There are countless options for the business owner. The only requirement is that within each class category created, it must be equal. Meaning, if a business owner pays one full time employee $200 a month, they cannot pay another same class employee only $100 a month. The reimbursement must be equal amounts within its employee class category. Here are some of the most popular class categories based on legitimate job differences:

- ⅄ full-time employees
- ⅄ part-time employees
- ⅄ Job Title
- ⅄ Length of employment
- ⅄ Geography

Depending on how much the business owner allocates to each employee by the end of the year, the tax deductions could potentially wash out the cost of the penalty. Plus, the employer benefits from paying this expense every month unlike the "penalty only" option. Not only does the business owner get a tax deduction, but the employee could potentially get double subsidy to help pay for their health insurance.

This becomes a win-win scenario for both parties. Now the business owner has a powerful recruitment and retention tool to attract and keep good employees. As you can see, this is a very powerful tool for a business owner as we are ushered into this new era of health insurance reform.

CHAPTER 12:
CONCLUSION

I want to thank you for taking the time to learn more about the evolution we are going to experience with ObamaCare. No matter what side of the fence you are on, your life is going to be affected by the changes in our health care system. For anyone suffering from pre-existing conditions, ObamaCare provides hope. For those who are struggling day by day financially, you now have an option for coverage with Medicaid. However, for a majority of Americans, estimates show we will be paying more than ever for our medical care. Not only will we be paying more in our monthly premiums, but also in sub-standard care because of Medicaid, higher taxes, fees, and economic consequences caused by this health reform law.

The good news is you have options! We have learned some ways we can save money on our taxes by wise investment choices. There are alternative "off-exchange" health insurance plans that provide excellent coverage, yet at a fraction of the cost. Plus, we learned about the HRA, the business owner's secret weapon for creating a win-win scenario. The HRA provides increased savings for the employee and creates an avenue for tax deductions which can virtually wash out the mandated penalty for employers.

We have hope. The sky is not going to fall. Hopefully this book will cause you to investigate these options further. Call your accountant! Call your financial planner! Call your local health insurance agent! Call your state's department of insurance. Feel free to call me. Any of these professionals are qualified to guide you in these important decisions.

Thank you again for your interest and time investigating ObamaCare. I am humbled at this opportunity to share with you these techniques to saving money. In an effort to keep you up-to-date on the upcoming changes please visit: http://www.SurvivingObamaCare.info and receive email alerts on the on going saga of ObamaCare.

REFERENCES

1. Himmelstein, David, Elizabeth Warren, Deborah Thorne, and Steffie Woolhandler, "MarketWatch: Illness and Injury as Contributors to Bankruptcy," *Health Affairs*, February 2005, 5 May 2005.

2. HuffintonPost: "Applying for Obamacare May Be As Difficult As Doing Taxes And 'Enormously Time Consuming", March 13, 2013

3. Wall Street Journal: "Health Reform Could Harm Medicaid Patients", Dec. 2009

4. Heritage Foundation, "Medicaid Provides Poor Quality Care: What the Research Shows", May 2011.

5. http://obamacarefacts.com/obamacare-taxes.php

6. National Review Online: "ObamaCare: Nothing To Brag About", February 2013.

7. http://healthreform.kff.org/en/the-basics/requirement-to-buy-coverage-flowchart.aspx

8. http://www.ncpa.org/pdfs/What-Does-Health-Reform-Mean-to-You.pdf

9. Milliman Health Care Exchange Issue Brief: "ACA Impact on Premium Rates in Individual and Small Group Market"

10. Congressional Budget Office letter to Senator Olympia Snowe, January 11, 2010.

Other Resources:

⅄ http://energycommerce.house.gov/sites/republicans.energycommerce.house.gov/files/analysis/20130305PremiumReport.pdf

⅄ http://americanactionforum.org/sites/default/files/AAF_Premiums_and_ACA_Survey.pdf

⅄ http://www.nytimes.com/2013/01/31/us/politics/irs-to-base-insurance-affordability-on-single-coverage.html?emc=tnt&tntemail0=y&_r=0

⅄ http://www.kff.org/healthreform/upload/8061.pdf/

⅄ ObamaCare: Projected Rate Increases By State:

State	Premium Increase	State	Premium Increase
Alabama	61%	Montana	61%
Alaska	30% to 80%	Nebraska	61%
Arizona	65% to 100%	Nevada	50% to 56%
Arkansas	61% to 100%	New Hampshire	19% to 39%
California	42% to 61%	New Jersey	39%
Colorado	19% to 41%	New Mexico	56%
Connecticut	39% to 64%	New York	***
Delaware	61%	North Carolina	61%
Florida	61%	North Dakota	56%
Georgia	61% to 100%	Ohio	55% to 106%
Hawaii	56%	Oklahoma	65% to 100%
Idaho	65% to 100%	Oregon	27% to 55%
Illinois	61%	Pennsylvania	39%
Indiana	61% to 106%	Rhode Island	8% to 39%
Iowa	56% to 100%	South Carolina	61% to 106%
Kansas	61%	South Dakota	56%
Kentucky	65% to 106%	Tennessee	61% to 100%
Louisiana	56%	Texas	35% to 65%
Maine	40%	Utah	56% to 90%
Maryland	34% to 39%	Vermont	***
Massachusetts	39%	Viginia	75% to 82%
Michigan	35% to 65%	Washington	39%
Minnesota	29% to 56%	West Virginia	56%
Mississippi	61%	Wisconsin	34% to 106%
Missouri	61% to 106%	Wyoming	61% to 100%

***Since these states already hyper regulate their insurance market,
Their significantly higher premiums are unlikely to change.

Sources:

http://blog.heritage.org/2013/03/18/obamacare-projected-premium-increases-by-state/

http://energycommerce.house.gov/sites/republicans.energycommerce.house.gov/files/analysis/20130305PremiumReport.pdf

ABOUT THE AUTHOR

Matthew Irons lives in sunny Arizona with his beautiful wife and two adorable little girls. Matthew is a licensed agent in multiple states helping his clients find quality health insurance that is affordable. Matthew is the agent/owner of Irons Family Insurance and provides solid plan solutions for this new era of health reform. If you have any questions or need assistance you are welcome to schedule an appointment to evaluate your needs.

To Learn More Visit:
www.IronsFamilyInsurance.com

Thank you again for reading this book. If you have found this information helpful please visit: www.amazon.com and leave a 5 star review.

*****

Thank You!

MATTHEW IRONS

SURVIVING OBAMACARE

www.ingramcontent.com/pod-product-compliance
Lightning Source LLC
Chambersburg PA
CBHW060633280326
41933CB00012B/2025